hors d'oeuvres

THE ESSENTIAL KITCHEN

hors d'oeuvres

VICKI LILEY

PERIPLUS

contents

Introduction 6

Step-by-step Techniques 8
Lemon and lime zest curls • Garnishes • Toast cups
• Fresh Asian rolls

Quick and Easy 12
Salt-and-spice almonds • Garlic-chili green olives • Crisp vegetable chips • Parmesan stars and hearts
• Parmesan wafers • Warm chorizo on crostini • Oysters in bacon
• Oven-roasted potatoes with lumpfish caviar

Dips and Dunks 24
Smoked trout pâté • Potted shrimp • White bean dip with herb toast fingers
• Curried mango dip • Skordalia

Tiny Morsels 34
Blini bites with salmon roe • Onion-and-chervil scones • Mini pissaladière
• Chicken drummettes • Sun-dried tomato–filled toast cups • Petite corn-and-herb muffins

Rolls and Wraps 46
Endive leaves with herbed cheese and walnuts • Melon and prosciutto wraps
• Fresh figs wrapped in prosciutto • Asparagus, ham and hollandaise rolls
• Continental sausage rolls

Meze to Tapas 54
Chilled gazpacho sips • Anchovy-filled zucchini flowers • Phyllo-wrapped shrimp with taramasalata
• Tuna with green olive salsa • Asparagus frittata

Skewered and Threaded 64

Chicken yakitori • Herb polenta baked in prosciutto
• Cherry tomato, bocconcini and basil skewers • Chili-herb shrimp • Skewered lamb and potatoes

Asian Bites 74

Tiny Peking duck rolls • Fresh Asian spring rolls • Steamed shrimp and spinach dumplings
• Cilantro and lime fish cakes • Cucumber disks with chili shrimp

Pastry and Breads 84

Pears and prosciutto on grilled bread • Cilantro and shrimp toasts • Herbed egg tartlets
• Ham rarebit toasts with dill pickle • Palmiers and pinwheels

Sweet Treats 94

Mascarpone and fruit tartlets • Fairy ice-cream sandwiches • Raspberry madeleines • Choc-almond apricots

Extras 102

Pesto • Tapenade • Taramasalata

Glossary 106

Index 108

Guide to Weights and Measures 111

hors d'oeuvres

introduction

Hors d'oeuvres are the heart of every party or get-together. Light, tempting and full of flavor, they are traditionally served with drinks. But you don't need to have a party to enjoy delicious bites of food. Hors d'oeuvres are ideal for breakfast or brunch nibbles, or for lunch or dinner snacks, and they can be packed into a picnic basket and served at an impromptu barbecue or a small gathering of friends or family. Enticing morsels of food are welcome whatever the occasion or time and will make any event more enjoyable and memorable.

If you are planning for a party, remember that people generally like to eat hot and filling foods in the winter, but may prefer light, cold hors d'oeuvres in the summer months. It's good to plan your hors d'oeuvres menu by calculating four to six bite-sized servings per person for each hour you anticipate the gathering or occasion will last. You can offer fewer servings for larger finger foods, and it's a good idea to have back-up foods for unexpectedly large appetites.

When planning, remember that simple things work best and make the most of what is in season. Four to five different hors d'oeuvres, made in multiples and displayed in lines on large platters, will look magnificent and will certainly be within the budget. Plan a contrast of textures, such as soft and crisp or smooth and rough, and include a variety of colors and flavors. A combination of the salt-and-spice almonds recipe in this book together with the garlic-chili green olives or chicken drummettes combined with warm chorizo on crostini, are delicious combinations which provide great textures, flavors and colors.

This book will give you the confidence to cater for any guest or friend, because of the wonderful variety of recipes available. It shows you how to make quick-and-easy finger foods, delectable dips and hors d'oeuvres that are rolled or wrapped or prepared and then served on skewers. You'll also enjoy the pastries and breads and mouth-watering sweet treats. This collection of recipes inspired by cuisines around the world includes Asian bites, Spanish tapas and the Mediterranean hors d'oeuvres known as meze.

From the recipe selection to the preparation tips, you'll discover everything you need to guarantee a wonderful and successful party.

Happy cooking!

Lemon and lime zest curls

see page 82 for cucumber disks with chili shrimp recipe

1   Using a citrus zester, firmly scrape the zest from lemons, limes, oranges or grapefruits. Use the zest to garnish and flavor your favorite recipes. If a zester is unavailable, remove zest with a vegetable peeler.

2   Remove any white pith from zest pieces.

3   Using a very sharp knife, finely slice zest. Place zest in a bowl of ice water. Refrigerate until zest curls, about 15 minutes. (If you are using a zester, it is generally not necessary to place zest in ice water.)

Garnishes

Scallion brushes and scallion curls

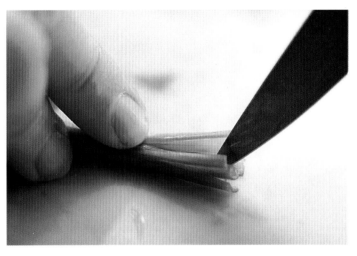

1 Using a sharp knife, remove the root section from each scallion (shallot/spring onion). Cut the paler green section of each scallion into 2-inch (5-cm) sections. Discard the darker green section, or save for another use.

2 To make scallion brushes: Make ¼ inch (6 mm) cuts in each scallion piece, forming a fringe.

3 To make scallion curls: Slice scallion pieces lengthwise into fine strips.

4 Place scallion brushes or strips in a bowl of ice water. Refrigerate until scallions curl, about 15 minutes. Drain and use to garnish or flavor your favorite recipes.

Toast cups

see page 42 for sun-dried tomato-filled toast cups recipe

1 Remove crusts using a serrated bread knife, then roll bread flat using a rolling pin.

2 Cut rounds from bread using a 2-inch (5-cm) cookie (pastry) cutter.

3 Brush one side of bread rounds with olive oil.

4 Press bread rounds into greased mini muffin pans. Bake at 375°F (190°C/Gas 5) until golden and crisp, 5–7 minutes. Remove pans from oven. Remove toast cups from pans and allow to cool.

Fresh Asian rolls

see page 76 for fresh Asian spring rolls recipe

1   Cover a work surface with a damp kitchen towel. Dip one rice paper wrapper at a time into a bowl of hot water. Allow each wrapper to soften, about 15 seconds.

2   Place softened rice paper wrappers onto damp towel. Spoon a small amount of filling into the middle of each wrapper.

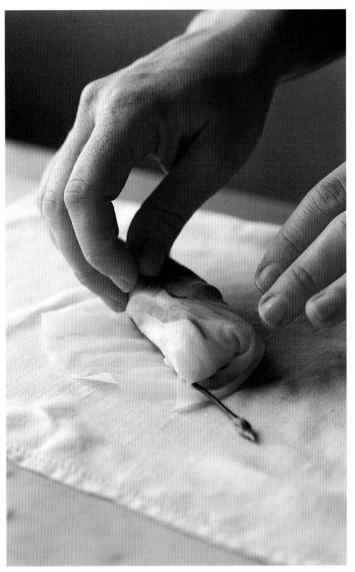

3   Fold edges over and roll up. Repeat with remaining ingredients. Cover rolls with a damp towel until ready to serve.

easy

Salt-and-spice almonds

6 tablespoons vegetable oil

14 oz (440 g) whole blanched almonds

2 tablespoons sea salt

1/2 teaspoon ground cayenne pepper, or to taste

In a medium frying pan over medium heat, warm oil. Add almonds and cook, tossing or stirring constantly, until they just become golden, 1–2 minutes. Be careful; almonds can burn easily at the last minute.

Combine sea salt and cayenne pepper in a bowl. Add hot almonds and toss until well coated. Place almonds on a parchment-lined (baking paper–lined) baking sheet and allow to cool.

Serve with drinks.

The almonds can be made 3–4 days ahead. Once completely cool, store in an airtight container.

Serves 3–4

Garlic-chili green olives

1/2 cup (4 fl oz/125 ml) virgin olive oil

4 cloves garlic, crushed

2 tablespoons balsamic vinegar

2 small red chili peppers, seeded and chopped

1 lb (500 g) good-quality whole green olives

In a bowl, combine oil, garlic, vinegar and chili peppers. Mix well. Add olives and stir until well coated. Cover and refrigerate overnight. Drain before serving.

The olives can marinate 2–3 days ahead. Keep covered and refrigerated.

Serves 3–4

Crisp vegetable chips

6 cups (48 fl oz/1.5 L) vegetable oil

3 sweet potatoes (kumaras), peeled

4 potatoes, peeled

4 parsnips, peeled

3 beets (beetroots), peeled

5 teaspoons sea salt, or to taste

Heat oil in a large, deep, heavy-bottomed saucepan or deep-fat fryer until it reaches 375°F (190°C) on a deep-frying thermometer, or until a small cube of bread dropped into the oil sizzles and turns golden. Working with one vegetable at a time (reserve beets until last as they color the oil red), thinly slice each vegetable using a vegetable peeler or mandoline.

Working with handful-sized batches, add vegetable slices to hot oil and deep-fry until golden, about 1 minute. Using a slotted spoon, remove from oil and drain on paper towels.

Sprinkle the chips liberally with sea salt and serve immediately.

Serves 6–8

Hint

Best prepared and cooked just before serving.

Parmesan stars and hearts

10 slices white sandwich bread

olive oil, for brushing

4 oz (125 g) freshly grated parmesan cheese

sea salt to taste

Preheat oven to 400°F (200°C/Gas 6). Using 2-inch (5-cm) star and heart cookie (pastry) cutters, press out shapes in each slice of bread. Brush one side with olive oil and place shapes, oiled side up, on a parchment-lined (baking paper–lined) baking sheet. Spoon grated parmesan onto oiled side of bread, covering bread as well as possible, then sprinkle with sea salt.

Cook in preheated oven until golden, 7–10 minutes. Keep an eye on the shapes while they bake, as they can burn very quickly.

Serve hot, warm, or at room temperature.

Makes about 30

Hints

Can be stored for 2 days in an airtight container, or frozen for up to 1 month.

PARMESAN STARS AND HEARTS

Parmesan wafers

10 oz (300 g) freshly grated parmesan cheese

Preheat oven to 350°F (180°C/Gas 4). Working in batches, place tablespoonfuls of cheese onto parchment-lined (baking paper–lined) baking sheets, allowing space for spreading. Flatten each cheese mound into a 2-inch (5-cm) round, or until it is almost paper thin. Bake until golden, 8–10 minutes. Remove baking sheets from oven. Using a metal spatula, remove wafers from sheets and place on a parchment-lined (baking paper–lined) rolling pin or similar curved shape. Allow to cool.

Serve warm or at room temperature.

Makes about 20

Hint

Can be stored for 1 day in an airtight container.

PARMESAN WAFERS   1 9

Warm chorizo on crostini

2 long loaves French bread or 2 baguettes

4 chorizo sausages

toothpicks

Cut bread into 24 slices ½ inch (12 mm) thick. Toast both sides of bread under a preheated broiler (grill) until golden and crisp. Cut each sausage into 6 slices, about ½ inch (12 mm) thick.

Heat a nonstick frying pan over medium heat. Fry chorizo sausage slices until lightly golden and heated through, about 4 minutes. Secure each piece of sausage to a slice of toast with a toothpick.

Serve immediately.

Makes 24

Hint

Bread can be toasted ahead of time.

Oysters in bacon

20 fresh oysters, shucked

¹/₄ cup (2 fl oz/60 ml) Worcestershire or other spicy sauce

freshly ground black pepper

10 slices good-quality bacon

toothpicks

Preheat oven to 375°F (190°C/Gas 5). Make sure oysters are free of any fragments of shell. Place oysters, Worcestershire sauce and pepper in a bowl. Cover and refrigerate for 2 hours. Place bacon on a work surface, and cut each slice in half. Arrange an oyster on each piece of bacon, roll up and secure with a toothpick. Place on a parchment-lined (baking paper–lined) baking sheet and bake in preheated oven for 10 minutes. Remove from oven and allow to cool a little.

Serve warm.

Makes 20

Hint

Can be prepared 2 hours before cooking.

WARM CHORIZO ON CROSTINI

Oven-roasted potatoes with lumpfish caviar

3 tablespoons olive oil

2 cloves garlic, crushed

3 teaspoons sea salt

24 small new potatoes, scrubbed

4 oz (125 g) crème fraîche or sour cream

1 oz (30 g) black lumpfish caviar

Preheat oven to 400°F (200°C/Gas 6). Combine oil, garlic and salt in a bowl. Toss potatoes in oil mixture. Arrange in a single layer on a parchment-lined (baking paper–lined) baking pan. Bake in preheated oven for 20–25 minutes, tossing occasionally, until potatoes are golden and tender when pierced with a sharp knife. Remove from oven and allow to cool for 5 minutes.

Using a sharp knife, cut a cross in the top of each potato, and press open slightly. Place potatoes on a serving platter. Top each with 1 teaspoon of crème fraîche, then garnish with lumpfish caviar.

Serve immediately.

Hint

Best made just before serving.

OVEN-ROASTED POTATOES WITH LUMPFISH CAVIAR

Smoked trout pâté

3 tablespoons butter

1 bunch chives, trimmed and snipped

2 smoked trout

3 hard-boiled eggs

1 teaspoon Thai sweet chili sauce

3 tablespoons good-quality mayonnaise

juice of 1 lemon

sea salt and freshly ground black pepper to taste

FOR SEEDED LAVASH TOAST

6 pieces lavash bread

olive oil, for brushing

mixed seeds such as sesame and poppy and/or
  cracked black pepper

Melt butter in a small saucepan over medium heat. Add chives and cook for 1 minute, then remove from heat and set aside. Remove skin from trout and carefully take flesh away from bone. Place trout, eggs, chili sauce, mayonnaise and lemon juice in a food processor and process until smooth. Season to taste with salt and pepper. Transfer to a bowl and fold in chive and butter mixture. Refrigerate until ready to serve.

Serve chilled with seeded lavash toast.

To make seeded lavash toast: Preheat oven to 375°F (190°C/Gas 5). Cut lavash bread into triangles. Brush lightly with oil and place, oiled side up, in a single layer on parchment-lined (baking paper–lined) baking sheets. Sprinkle with seeds and/or cracked black pepper. Bake in preheated oven until golden, 6–8 minutes.

Serve hot or cold.

Serves 10

Hints

Pâté can be made 1 day ahead. Keep covered in refrigerator.

SMOKED TROUT PÂTÉ

Potted shrimp

6½ oz (200 g) unsalted butter

2 lb (1 kg) cooked shrimp (prawns), peeled and deveined

⅔ cup (5 fl oz/150 ml) olive oil

½ teaspoon white pepper

juice of 1 lime

1 bunch basil (1 cup/1 oz/30 g leaves), roughly chopped

sea salt to taste

FOR WHOLE-GRAIN TOAST TRIANGLES

12 slices whole-grain bread

olive oil, for brushing

Clarify butter by melting it in a saucepan over low heat. Remove from heat and allow to cool a little. Spoon liquid from top and leave fatty solids in bottom of saucepan. Place shrimp and olive oil in a food processor and process to form a smooth paste. Add pepper, lime juice and basil, then process for another 30 seconds.

Spoon into 2 straight-sided dishes with a 1½-cup (12 fl oz/375 ml) capacity. Spoon a little clarified butter over the top of each. Refrigerate for 1 hour.

Serve with whole-grain toast triangles.

To make whole-grain toast triangles: Preheat oven to 400°F (200°C/Gas 6). Remove crusts from bread. Brush each slice lightly with olive oil, then cut into 4 triangles. Place, oiled side up, in a single layer on a parchment-lined (baking paper–lined) baking sheet and bake in preheated oven until crisp and golden, about 7 minutes.

Serves 10

Hints

Potted shrimp and toasts can be made 1 day ahead. Keep potted shrimp covered in the refrigerator, and store toast triangles in an airtight container.

POTTED SHRIMP

White bean dip with herb toast fingers

2 cloves garlic, chopped

1 small red (Spanish) onion, chopped

10 oz (300 g) can cannelloni beans, drained and
 rinsed

2 tablespoons chopped fresh parsley

1 tablespoon olive oil

juice of $\frac{1}{2}$ lemon

sea salt and freshly ground black pepper to taste

1 teaspoon extra virgin olive oil, for serving

FOR HERB TOAST FINGERS

1 loaf focaccia bread, thinly sliced

olive oil, for brushing

$\frac{1}{2}$ cup ($\frac{3}{4}$ oz/20 g) chopped fresh herbs of choice
 such as rosemary, thyme, parsley and dill

sea salt to taste

Place garlic, onion and beans in a food processor and process until smooth. Add parsley, oil and lemon juice and process until well combined, about 10 seconds. Season to taste with salt and pepper. Spoon into 1 serving bowl or 2 smaller bowls. Cover and refrigerate until ready to serve. Just before serving, drizzle with extra virgin olive oil.

Serve with herb toast fingers.

To make herb toast fingers: Preheat oven to 400°F (200°C/Gas 6). Brush one side of each bread slice with olive oil, sprinkle generously with herbs, then top with a sprinkling of sea salt. Bake in preheated oven until golden and crisp, about 7 minutes.

Serve hot or at room temperature.

Serves 10

Hints

White bean dip and herb toast fingers can be made 1 day ahead. Cover and refrigerate dip, and store toasts in an airtight container.

WHITE BEAN DIP WITH HERB TOAST FINGERS

Curried mango dip

1 tablespoon vegetable oil

1 onion, finely chopped

1 teaspoon mild curry powder

10 oz (300 g) plain (natural) yogurt

2 tablespoons mango chutney

mixed fresh vegetables and baby pappadams, for
  serving

Heat oil in a small frying pan over medium heat. Add onion and cook until softened, about 1 minute. Stir in curry powder and cook until aromatic, about 1 minute. Remove pan from heat, and allow to cool. Gently stir in yogurt and mango chutney. Spoon into a serving bowl, place in center of a platter and surround with vegetables such as Belgian endive (chicory) leaves, slices of carrot, celery, red and green bell peppers (capsicums), English (hothouse) cucumber, blanched cauliflower florets and blanched asparagus spears. If desired, fry the pappadams in hot vegetable oil or microwave on high according to directions on package.

Serves 4–6

Hints

Dip can be made 1 day ahead. Keep covered and refrigerated.

CURRIED MANGO DIP   3 1

Skordalia

4 large potatoes, peeled and diced

4 cloves garlic, finely chopped

2 teaspoons sea salt

juice of 1 lemon

1/2 cup (4 fl oz /125 ml) virgin olive oil

mixed crisp, fresh salad vegetables such as
   whole radishes, celery sticks and carrot pieces,
   for serving

Cook potatoes in a large saucepan of boiling salted water until tender, about 8 minutes. Drain and mash. Add garlic, salt and lemon juice, and mix well. Gradually add olive oil in a fine drizzle until incorporated. If the mashed potatoes are too dry, add more olive oil.

Serve warm with vegetables.

Serves 6–8

Hints

Skordalia is best when made just before serving. It can also be accompanied by grilled asparagus spears and zucchini (courgette) slices.

Blini bites with salmon roe

1¼ cups (6½ oz/200 g) self-rising flour

pinch baking soda (bicarbonate of soda)

1 egg, beaten

¾ cup (6 fl oz/180 ml) milk

1 tablespoon grated white onion

sea salt and freshly ground black pepper to taste

2 tablespoons butter, melted

½ cup (4 oz/125 g) crème fraîche or sour cream

4 oz (125 g) salmon roe

Place flour and baking soda in a food processor. Add egg and milk. Process until smooth. Transfer batter to a bowl. Add grated onion, salt and pepper. Mix well. Cover and let stand for 10 minutes.

Heat a frying pan over medium heat, and brush with melted butter. Drop batter by the tablespoonful into hot pan. Cook until golden, about 1 minute per side. Remove from pan and allow to cool to room temperature.

Just before serving, top each blini with crème fraîche and a small amount of salmon roe.

Makes about 24

Hints

Blinis can be frozen for up to 3 weeks. Substitute smoked salmon or steamed asparagus tips for salmon roe for a taste variation.

BLINI BITES WITH SALMON ROE

Onion-and-chervil scones

2 cups (8 oz/250 g) self-rising flour, sifted

1 tablespoon butter, chopped into small pieces

1 tablespoon grated white onion

2 tablespoons chopped fresh chervil

pinch sea salt

8 fl oz (250 ml) buttermilk

$^1/_2$ cup (4 oz/125 g) crème fraîche

3 oz (90 g) sliced smoked salmon, cut into

 $^1/_2$-inch (12-mm) strips

chervil sprigs, for garnish

Preheat oven to 425°F (220°C/Gas 7). Place flour in a bowl. Using your fingertips, rub butter into flour until mixture resembles fine bread-crumbs. Stir in onion, chopped chervil and salt. Add enough buttermilk to form a soft, sticky dough. Turn dough out onto a floured work surface. Press or roll to a ¾-inch (2-cm) thickness. Cut into rounds using a 2-inch (5-cm) floured cookie (pastry) cutter. Place scones on a parchment-lined (baking paper–lined) baking sheet. Bake in preheated oven until golden, 12–15 minutes. Remove baking sheet from oven and turn scones onto a clean, dry kitchen towel. Wrap towel around scones until ready to serve.

To serve: Split each scone in half horizontally. Place 1 teaspoon of crème fraîche on each half and top with salmon and chervil. Serve immediately.

Makes about 16

Hint

Scones can be baked ahead and frozen for up to

3 weeks.

Mini pissaladière

2 sheets frozen pre-rolled puff pastry, thawed

¼ cup (2 fl oz/60 ml) olive oil

1½ lb (750 g) yellow (brown) onions, thinly sliced

2 oz (60 g) anchovy fillets

4 oz (125 g) pitted black olives

24 tiny whole basil leaves, for garnish

Preheat oven to 350°F (180°C/Gas 4). Place puff pastry sheets on a floured work surface. Using a floured 2-inch (5-cm) cookie (pastry) cutter, cut out 24 rounds. Place on a parchment-lined (baking paper–lined) baking sheet and cover with plastic wrap while cooking onion topping.

Warm oil in a heavy-bottomed frying pan over medium heat. Add onions and cook over medium–low heat until soft and slightly browned, about 10 minutes. Remove frying pan from heat and allow onions to cool.

Top each pastry round with onion mixture. Halve the anchovy fillets lengthwise and place two halves in a cross pattern on top of onions on each pastry round. Cut olives into slivers and place in angles of anchovy crosses. Bake until pastry is golden and crisp, 7–10 minutes.

Serve hot, garnished with basil leaves.

Makes 24

Hints

Onions can be prepared 2 hours ahead, but pastry is best baked just before serving.

MINI PISSALADIÈRE

Chicken drummettes

24 small chicken wings

2 tablespoons vegetable oil

3 tablespoons hoisin sauce

4 tablespoons light soy sauce

2 tablespoons dry sherry

4 cloves garlic, crushed

1 small red chili pepper, seeded and chopped

3 teaspoons peeled and grated fresh ginger

$^{1}/_{2}$ cup (4 fl oz/125 ml) hoisin sauce, for dipping

Cut chicken wings in half at main joint. Discard wing tips (or use for making stock). With a sharp knife, trim meat around each cut joint, then scrape meat down bone and push it over bottom joint so that wing resembles a small chicken leg. Place drummettes in a shallow dish.

Combine oil, 3 tablespoons hoisin sauce, soy sauce, sherry, garlic, chili and ginger in a screw-top jar. Shake until well combined. Pour over chicken. Cover and marinate in refrigerator for 3 hours.

Preheat oven to 350°F (180°C/Gas 4). Remove chicken from marinade and place in a lightly greased baking dish. Bake in preheated oven until tender, 15–20 minutes.

Serve hot or cold, with hoisin sauce for dipping.

Makes 24

CHICKEN DRUMMETTES

Sun-dried tomato-filled toast cups

(see page 10 for step-by-step instructions)

15 large slices white sandwich bread

olive oil, for brushing

4 oz (125 g) sun-dried tomatoes in oil, drained
  and chopped

4 oz (125 g) freshly grated parmesan cheese

10 oz (300 g) ricotta cheese

2 tablespoons chopped fresh parsley

sea salt and freshly ground black pepper to taste

small herb leaves such as basil, parsley or thyme,
  for garnish

Preheat oven to 375°F (190°C/Gas 5). Remove crusts from bread with a serrated bread knife. Roll bread flat using a rolling pin. Cut rounds from bread using a 2-inch (5-cm) cookie (pastry) cutter. Brush one side of bread rounds with oil. Press bread rounds, oiled side up, into greased mini muffin pans. Bake in preheated oven until golden and crisp, 5–7 minutes. Remove pans from oven, then remove toast cups from pans and allow to cool.

Meanwhile, prepare filling: In a bowl, combine sun-dried tomatoes, parmesan, ricotta, parsley, salt and pepper. Mix until well combined.

Spoon cheese mixture into toast cups, and garnish with herb leaves.

Makes 30

Hints

Toast cups can be made ahead of time, and either frozen for up to 1 month or kept in an airtight container for up to 1 week. Sun-dried tomato filling can be made 2 hours ahead. Keep it covered in the refrigerator.

Petite corn-and-herb muffins

½ cup (2½ oz/75 g) all-purpose flour

⅓ cup (3 oz/90 g) fine cornmeal

1 teaspoon baking powder

pinch sea salt

freshly ground black pepper to taste

2 tablespoons butter, melted

1 egg, beaten

3 tablespoons milk

1 small red chili pepper, seeded and chopped

1 tablespoon chopped fresh cilantro (fresh
  coriander)

1 tablespoon chopped fresh basil

FOR HERB AND GARLIC BUTTER

4 oz (125 g) butter, softened

1 clove garlic, crushed

2 tablespoons chopped fresh basil

1 teaspoon lime juice

Preheat oven to 350°F (180°C/Gas 4). Sift flour into a bowl. Stir in cornmeal, baking powder, salt and pepper. Make a well in center of dry ingredients. Quickly fold in butter, egg, milk, chili, cilantro and basil. Mix until just combined. Spoon into 12 greased mini muffin pans. Bake in preheated oven until golden, about 12 minutes. Remove pans from oven, and turn muffins out onto a wire rack.

Serve warm, split in half and spread with herb and garlic butter.

To make herb and garlic butter: In a small bowl, combine butter, garlic, basil and lime juice. Mix well.

Makes 12

Hints

Muffins are best made and eaten warm on the same day as baking. Herb and garlic butter can be made 1 day ahead. Keep covered and refrigerated.

PETITE CORN-AND-HERB MUFFINS

Endive leaves with herbed cheese and walnuts

4 heads Belgian endive (chicory/witloof)

8 oz (250 g) ricotta cheese

$^1/_4$ cup ($^1/_3$ oz/10 g) chopped fresh parsley

$^1/_4$ cup ($^1/_3$ oz/10 g) chopped fresh dill

1 garlic clove, crushed

freshly ground black pepper to taste

walnut pieces, for garnish

Separate Belgian endive leaves, then wash and pat dry with paper towels. Trim bottom of each leaf. Using a wooden spoon or fork, blend ricotta, parsley, dill, garlic and pepper in a small bowl. Spoon a small amount on each leaf — not too much to make it difficult for the leaf to hold the filling.

Garnish with walnut pieces and serve.

Serves 8–10

Hints

Ricotta filling can be made 2 hours ahead. Assemble dish just before serving.

Melon and prosciutto wraps

¹/₂ cantaloupe

¹/₂ honeydew melon

24 very thin slices prosciutto

48 toothpicks

Scoop out seeds from each melon half. Cut each half into 6 wedges. Remove melon skins. Wrap 1 or 2 slices of prosciutto around each wedge. Secure prosciutto with 4 toothpicks. Cut each wedge into 4 bite-sized pieces. Cover and refrigerate.

Serve chilled.

Makes 48

Fresh figs wrapped in prosciutto

6 large ripe figs

freshly ground black pepper to taste

24 very thin slices prosciutto

24 toothpicks

Wash and dry figs, taking care not to bruise the delicate fruit. Cut each fig into quarters. Grind a little black pepper onto each quarter. Wrap in a slice of prosciutto. Secure prosciutto with a toothpick. Cover and refrigerate.

Serve chilled.

Makes 24

Hints

Can be made 2–3 hours ahead of time and chilled.

Make sure both melon wedges and figs are well wrapped so that they do not dry out.

MELON AND PROSCIUTTO WRAPS

Asparagus, ham and hollandaise rolls

FOR CREPES

1 cup (5 oz/150 g) all-purpose flour

½ teaspoon sea salt

2 eggs

2 egg yolks

1¼ cups (10 fl oz/300 ml) milk

1 tablespoon melted butter

melted butter, for cooking

10 asparagus spears

8 fl oz (250 ml) prepared hollandaise sauce (sold at supermarkets and delicatessens)

10 thin slices ham

To make the crepes: Sift flour and salt into a bowl. Make a well in center. In another bowl, combine eggs, yolks, milk and 1 tablespoon melted butter. Pour into well in flour mixture. Mix with a wooden spoon or balloon whisk until batter is smooth. Pour batter into a small pitcher. Cover with plastic wrap and allow to stand for at least 30 minutes.

Brush bottom of an 8-inch (20-cm) crepe pan or frying pan with melted butter. Warm pan over medium heat for 1 minute. Pour a thin layer of crepe batter into pan and swirl to coat bottom evenly. Cook over medium heat until top of crepe is firm, about 3 minutes. Lift edge with a spatula, and when bottom is golden brown, flip crepe and brown second side. Repeat with remaining batter. Stack cooked crepes on a plate, separating them with parchment (baking paper).

Trim asparagus to 8-inch (20-cm) lengths. Blanch in a saucepan of boiling water for 2 minutes. Drain and refresh in cold water. Pat asparagus dry with paper towels.

Working with one crepe at a time, spread with 1 tablespoon of hollandaise, then top with a slice of ham and an asparagus spear. Firmly roll crepe and cut diagonally in half. Repeat with remaining ingredients.

Hint

Crepes can be made up to 6 hours ahead.

Makes 20

Continental sausage rolls

2 thick Continental (kransky) sausages

4 sheets frozen puff pastry, thawed

1 egg, beaten

2 teaspoons sesame seeds

$1/2$ cup (4 fl oz/125 ml) barbecue sauce or ketchup,
 for dipping

Preheat oven to 440°F (225°C/Gas 7½). Using a sharp knife, cut sausages lengthwise into 8 strips. Place 2 sheets of pastry on a work surface, and cut each sheet into 4 squares. Place a sausage strip on each pastry square, straight and in the middle. Using a pastry brush, brush edges of square with beaten egg. Roll each pastry once over sausage strip, forming a neat sausage roll. Do not double-roll pastry. Trim away any excess pastry (sausages vary in size, so there may be leftover pastry). Cut into bite-sized pieces, about 1 inch (2.5 cm) long. Place on parchment-lined (baking paper–lined) baking sheets, brush tops with beaten egg and sprinkle each piece with sesame seeds. Bake in preheated oven until golden and crisp, about 15 minutes.

Serve hot with barbecue sauce or ketchup for dipping.

Makes about 36

Hint

Rolls can be prepared 2 hours ahead, covered and refrigerated, then baked just before serving.

CONTINENTAL SAUSAGE ROLLS

Chilled gazpacho sips

1 English (hothouse) cucumber

1/2 red (Spanish) onion, chopped

1 ripe tomato, finely chopped

1/2 green bell pepper (capsicum), seeded and chopped

1/2 red bell pepper (capsicum), seeded and chopped

3 1/2 cups (28 fl oz/875 ml) canned tomato juice

1 teaspoon superfine sugar (caster sugar)

3 tablespoons dry white wine

3 cloves garlic, crushed

Cut cucumber in half lengthwise. Scoop out seeds, using a teaspoon. Finely chop one half of cucumber. Cut remaining half into thin slivers for garnish, cover and set aside.

Combine chopped cucumber, onion, tomato and bell peppers in a bowl and set aside.

Combine tomato juice, sugar, white wine and garlic in a pitcher. Chill for at least 2 hours, or until ready to serve.

To serve, pour juice mixture into 16 shot glasses, then spoon in vegetable mixture. Garnish each glass with a thin sliver of cucumber.

Makes 16 servings, about 1½ oz (45 ml) each.

Hint

Can be prepared up to 6 hours before serving.

CHILLED GAZPACHO SIPS

Anchovy-filled zucchini flowers

3/4 cup (4 oz/125 g) all-purpose flour

pinch sea salt

1 egg

1 tablespoon olive oil

3 fl oz (90 ml) beer

1 tablespoon chopped mixed fresh herbs

8 small zucchini (courgette) flowers

8 canned anchovy fillets, drained

3 cups (24 fl oz/750 ml) vegetable oil, for deep-
    frying

sea salt, for serving

Place flour and pinch of salt in a food processor. Add egg, oil, beer and herbs. Process until smooth, about 10 seconds. Transfer batter to a bowl. Cover and allow to stand for 10 minutes.

Meanwhile, clean zucchini flowers and trim zucchini section (not flower ends) to 1 inch (2.5 cm), otherwise zucchini will drop off during cooking. Carefully open each flower and insert an anchovy fillet. Press petals closed.

Preheat oven to 225°F (110°C/Gas ¼).

Heat oil in a large, deep, heavy-bottomed saucepan or deep-fat fryer until the temperature reaches 375°F (190°C) on a deep-frying thermometer, or until a small cube of bread dropped into the oil sizzles and turns golden. Working in batches, dip flowers into batter. Deep-fry in hot oil until golden and crisp, about 1 minute. Drain on paper towels. Keep warm in preheated oven. Repeat with remaining flowers.

Serve immediately with extra sea salt.

Makes 8

Hints

Best made just before serving, but batter can be prepared up to 30 minutes ahead (add more beer if batter becomes too thick).

ANCHOVY-FILLED ZUCCHINI FLOWERS

Phyllo-wrapped shrimp with taramasalata

8 sheets phyllo pastry

2¹/₂ oz (75 g) butter, melted

16 medium jumbo shrimp (medium green king prawns), peeled and deveined, tails intact

1 cup taramasalata (see recipe page 104)

Preheat oven to 400°F (200°C/Gas 6). Place one sheet of phyllo pastry on a work surface (keep remaining phyllo covered with a damp towel to prevent it from drying out). Brush sheet with melted butter. Place another phyllo sheet on top and brush with melted butter. Using a sharp knife or kitchen shears, cut the doubled sheet into 4 long strips. Place 1 teaspoon of taramasalata at one end of each strip, then top with a shrimp. Fold phyllo over shrimp to form a triangle (take one corner up to join opposite side of strip), allowing shrimp tail to protrude from one corner of triangle. Continue folding until shrimp is completely wrapped. Repeat with remaining ingredients.

Place triangles on parchment-lined (baking paper–lined) baking sheets. Brush tops with butter. Bake until pastry is golden and crisp, about 10 minutes.

Serve immediately.

Makes 16

Hint

Can be prepared 2 hours ahead.

PHYLLO-WRAPPED SHRIMP WITH TARAMASALATA

Tuna with green olive salsa

1 lb (500 g) tuna steaks, 1 inch (2.5 cm) thick

grated zest (rind) of 1 lemon

2 tablespoons extra virgin olive oil

3 cloves garlic, crushed

FOR GREEN OLIVE SALSA

2 canned anchovy fillets

$1/2$ cup (3 oz/90 g) pitted green olives, chopped

1 clove garlic, crushed

$1/3$ cup ($1/2$ oz/15 g) chopped fresh flat-leaf parsley

1 tablespoon white wine vinegar

1 tablespoon lemon juice

$1/4$ cup (2 fl oz/60 ml) virgin olive oil

toothpicks

Place tuna in a shallow glass or ceramic dish. In a small bowl, combine lemon zest, oil and garlic. Pour over tuna. Cover and refrigerate for 2 hours.

Meanwhile, to make salsa, mash anchovy fillets in a bowl, then add olives, garlic, parsley, vinegar, lemon juice and oil. Mix until well combined. Cover and chill until serving.

Preheat a broiler (grill) or prepare a fire in a grill. Remove tuna from marinade and cook for 1 minute on each side. Allow center of tuna to remain pink. Remove from heat and allow to cool.

Using a very sharp knife, cut tuna steaks into 1¼-inch (3-cm) cubes. Skewer each with a toothpick.

Top each cube with 1 teaspoon of green olive salsa, and serve with remaining salsa in a bowl alongside.

Serves 8

Hints

Best cooked just before serving. Tuna can marinate overnight. Salsa can be made 1 day ahead.

Asparagus frittata

1½ lb (750 g) asparagus

6 eggs, beaten

8 oz (250 g) cream cheese

3 tablespoons all-purpose flour

3 tablespoons freshly grated parmesan cheese

1 tablespoon chopped fresh dill

2 tablespoons chopped fresh flat-leaf parsley

sea salt and freshly ground black pepper to taste

Preheat oven to 340°F (175°C/Gas 3½). Trim asparagus spears to 8-inch (20-cm) lengths. Line a deep, 8-inch (20-cm) square cake pan with parchment (baking paper). Place asparagus spears in pan side by side, alternating tips and bases of stalks. (Do not place layers at right angles to each other.)

Place eggs, cream cheese, flour, parmesan, dill, parsley, salt and pepper in a food processor. Process until smooth. Pour over asparagus. Bake in preheated oven until firm to touch, 50–55 minutes. Remove from oven and allow to cool in pan, then cut into 24 pieces.

Serve chilled or at room temperature.

Makes 24

Hints

Can be made 1 day ahead. Cover and refrigerate.

Chicken yakitori

10 bamboo skewers

$^{1}/_{2}$ cup (4 fl oz/125 ml) soy sauce

$^{1}/_{2}$ cup (4 fl oz/125 ml) sake or dry sherry

2 teaspoons sugar

1 tablespoon peeled and grated fresh ginger

2 tablespoons snipped chives

2 lb (1 kg) chicken breast fillets

12 scallions (shallots/spring onions), dark green
   tops removed

olive oil, for brushing

$^{1}/_{2}$ cup (4 fl oz/125 ml) soy sauce, for dipping

Soak bamboo skewers in cold water for 10 minutes, then drain. Place soy sauce, sake, sugar, ginger and chives in a screw-top jar and shake well to mix.

Trim chicken breasts of any fat and membranes and cut into bite-sized cubes, about 1½ inches (4 cm). Place chicken cubes in a shallow glass or ceramic dish, pour marinade over cubes, cover and refrigerate for 1 hour.

Preheat a stovetop grill pan, broiler (grill), or barbecue.

Cut scallions into 2-inch (5-cm) lengths. Drain chicken, and thread cubes onto skewers alternately with scallions. Brush chicken and scallions with olive oil and cook until golden, about 5 minutes per side.

Serve hot with soy sauce for dipping.

Serves 10

Hints

Can be assembled 2 hours ahead. Then cook and serve.

CHICKEN YAKITORI

Herb polenta baked in prosciutto

12 oz (375 g) instant polenta

¹/₄ cup (¹/₄ oz/7 g) finely chopped fresh flat-leaf
  parsley

3 cloves garlic, crushed

¹/₄ cup (1 oz/30g) freshly grated parmesan cheese

2 oz (60 g) unsalted butter

10 short bamboo skewers

20 thin slices prosciutto

¹/₄ cup (1 oz/30 g) freshly grated parmesan cheese,
  for serving

Preheat oven to 375°F (190°C/Gas 5). Cook polenta according to instructions on package. When almost cooked, mix in parsley, garlic, parmesan and butter. Pour polenta into a lightly oiled pan measuring 11 inches by 7 inches by 2 inches (28 cm by 18 cm by 5 cm), and smooth surface with a spatula. Set aside to cool for about 1 hour.

Soak skewers in cold water for 10 minutes, then drain.

Turn polenta out onto a work surface and cut into 20 uniform, bite-sized cubes. Wrap each cube in a slice of prosciutto and thread 2 cubes onto each skewer. Place skewers on a parchment-lined (baking paper–lined) baking sheet. Bake in preheated oven until prosciutto is golden and crisp, about 20 minutes.

Serve hot, with a sprinkling of parmesan.

Makes 10

Hints

Can be prepared 2 hours ahead. Cover and refrigerate, then bake and serve.

HERB POLENTA BAKED IN PROSCIUTTO

Cherry tomato, bocconcini and basil skewers

24 cherry tomatoes

sea salt and freshly ground black pepper to taste

24 baby bocconcini

24 small basil leaves

24 short bamboo skewers

extra virgin olive oil, for serving

Cut cherry tomatoes in half and season with salt and pepper. To assemble, place a tomato half on a skewer, followed by a bocconcini, then a basil leaf and finally a second tomato half. Repeat with remaining ingredients and skewers.

Serve drizzled with olive oil.

Makes 24

Hints

Can be made 2–3 hours ahead of time and chilled.

Drizzle with oil just before serving.

CHERRY TOMATO, BOCCONCINI AND BASIL SKEWERS

Chili-herb shrimp

$^1/_3$ cup (3 fl oz/90 ml) olive oil

2 tablespoons peeled and chopped fresh ginger

2 garlic cloves, crushed

2 small pieces lemongrass, crushed

1 small red chili pepper, seeded and chopped

2 limes or lemons, juiced

$^1/_4$ cup ($^1/_3$ oz/10 g) chopped mixed fresh herbs of choice

4 lb (2 kg) jumbo shrimp (green king prawns), peeled and deveined

2 tablespoons olive oil, for cooking

20 short bamboo skewers

lime or lemon wedges, for garnish

In a large bowl, combine ⅓ cup olive oil, ginger, garlic, lemongrass, chili pepper, lime juice and herbs. Mix well. Add shrimp and toss until well coated in marinade. Cover with plastic wrap and refrigerate for 1 hour.

Warm 2 tablespoons oil in a frying pan over medium heat. Drain shrimp. Working in batches, fry shrimp until they just change color, 2–3 minutes.

Thread shrimp onto skewers and serve with lime or lemon wedges.

Serves 10

Hint

Best served immediately after cooking.

CHILI-HERB SHRIMP

Skewered lamb and potatoes

1 lb (500 g) ground (minced) lamb

1 tablespoon chopped fresh flat-leaf parsley

1 tablespoon chopped fresh mint

3 cloves garlic, minced

2 tablespoons dried breadcrumbs

sea salt and freshly ground black pepper to taste

2 tablespoons vegetable oil

13 oz (400 g) small or medium potatoes

2 tablespoons olive oil

24 mint leaves, for serving

24 short bamboo skewers

In a bowl, combine lamb, parsley, chopped mint, garlic, breadcrumbs, salt and pepper. With wet hands, mix until well combined. Roll mixture into bite-sized balls — you should be able to make about 24.

Warm vegetable oil in a frying pan over medium heat. Working in batches, cook lamb balls until brown on all sides, about 10 minutes. Shake pan occasionally to brown meatballs evenly. Remove from pan and drain on paper towels.

Preheat oven to 425°F (220°C/Gas 7).

Cut potatoes into bite-sized wedges, or cubes about 1 inch (2.5 cm). Toss in olive oil and season with salt and pepper. Place on a parchment-lined (baking paper–lined) baking sheet and bake until golden and crisp, 15–20 minutes.

Place a lamb ball, a potato wedge or cube and a mint leaf on each skewer. Repeat with remaining ingredients and skewers.

Makes 24

Hint

Best served immediately after cooking.

Tiny Peking duck rolls

1 Chinese roast duck (purchase fresh from Asian
markets)

12 scallions (shallots/spring onions) (see page 9
for step-by-step scallion brushes)

4 carrots, peeled and julienned

4 flour tortillas

48 toothpicks

1/2 cup (4 fl oz/125 ml) hoisin sauce, for dipping

Remove meat from duck and discard bones. Slice meat and skin into bite-sized pieces about 1 inch (2.5 cm).

Trim away root end of scallions, then cut scallions into 1¼-inch (3-cm) lengths. Using a sharp knife or kitchen shears, cut a fringe in end of each scallion. Place scallion brushes in a bowl of ice water (scallions will curl in ice water). Place carrots in bowl of ice water with scallions. Chill until ready to serve.

Warm tortillas in a microwave oven for 1 minute or wrapped in aluminum foil in a 275°F (140°C/Gas 1) oven for 10 minutes. Using kitchen shears, cut tortillas into ¾-inch by 4-inch (2-cm by 10-cm) strips.

Working in batches, place tortilla strips on work surface. Top each strip with a small amount of duck, 1 scallion curl, 4 to 5 carrot pieces and a dash of hoisin sauce. Roll up and secure with a toothpick.

Serve with hoisin sauce for dipping.

Makes about 48

Hints

Prepare duck, scallions and carrots 2 hours ahead.

Assemble just before serving.

TINY PEKING DUCK ROLLS

Fresh Asian spring rolls

(see page 11 for step-by-step instructions)

1½ oz (50 g) cellophane (bean thread) noodles

½ cup (2½ oz/ 75 g) julienned carrot

½ cup (2½ oz/ 75 g) julienned zucchini
  (courgette)

½ cup (2½ oz/ 75 g) julienned red bell pepper
  (capsicum)

6 scallions (shallots/spring onions), julienned

juice of 1 lime

2 tablespoons fish sauce

1 teaspoon peeled and grated ginger

¼ cup (⅓ oz/10 g) chopped fresh cilantro
  (coriander)

2 tablespoons Thai sweet chili sauce

¼ cup whole cilantro (coriander) leaves

16 round rice paper wrappers, 6 inches (15 cm) in
  diameter

16 cooked jumbo shrimp (king prawns), peeled
  and deveined

16 garlic chives

½ cup (4 fl oz/125 ml) Thai sweet chili sauce or
  soy sauce for dipping

Place noodles in a heatproof bowl and cover with boiling water. Allow to stand until softened, about 10 minutes, then drain.

In a bowl, combine carrot, zucchini, bell pepper, scallions, lime juice, fish sauce, ginger and chopped cilantro. Allow to stand for 10 minutes. Drain well, then place in a bowl. Add chili sauce and cilantro leaves and mix well.

Fill a bowl with warm water, and place a paper towel on a work surface. Dip a rice paper wrapper in hot water until soft, about 15 seconds, then place on paper towel. Spoon 1 tablespoon vegetable mixture in center of wrapper, top with a small amount of noodles, a shrimp and a garlic chive (allow chive to protrude above wrapper's edge), then roll wrapper into a cylinder. Cover prepared rolls with a damp kitchen towel to prevent them from drying out. Repeat with remaining ingredients.

Serve with Thai sweet chili sauce or soy sauce for dipping.

Makes 16

Hints

Can be prepared 1 hour ahead. Keep rolls covered and refrigerated.

Steamed shrimp and spinach dumplings

8 oz (250 g) jumbo shrimp (green king prawns), peeled and deveined

1 tablespoon vegetable oil

2 cloves garlic, crushed

1 cup (1 oz/30 g) packed spinach leaves, shredded

1 tablespoon finely chopped canned water chestnuts

2 scallions (shallots/spring onions), finely chopped

1 tablespoon light soy sauce

16 wonton wrappers

3 fl oz (90 ml) Thai sweet chili sauce or soy sauce, for dipping

Finely chop shrimp. Set aside. Heat oil in a wok or frying pan over medium heat. Add garlic and fry until aromatic, about 1 minute. Stir in spinach and chopped shrimp and stir-fry until shrimp change color, about 2 minutes. Remove from heat and allow to cool. Add water chestnuts, scallions and soy sauce to shrimp and spinach mixture. Mix until well combined.

Place wonton wrappers on a work surface and cover with a damp kitchen towel. Working with one wrapper at a time, lay wrapper on work surface and place 1 teaspoon shrimp filling in middle. Brush edges of wonton wrapper with water (use a pastry brush or a finger). Gather wonton corners together and twist to seal. Set aside and cover with plastic wrap. Repeat with remaining wonton wrappers and shrimp filling.

Line a medium bamboo steamer with parchment (baking paper). Half fill a medium wok with water (check water level with steamer in wok — steamer should not touch water). Bring water to a boil. Arrange filled wontons in steamer. Cover with lid. Place steamer over boiling water. Steam for 12 minutes, adding more water to wok if necessary. Lift steamer off wok and carefully remove dumplings.

Serve warm with Thai sweet chili sauce or soy sauce for dipping.

Makes 16

Hints

Dumpling filling can be prepared 2 hours ahead.

Keep covered and refrigerated.

STEAMED SHRIMP AND SPINACH DUMPLINGS

Cilantro and lime fish cakes

1 lb (500 g) redfish fillets or skinless, boneless
   white-fleshed fish fillets

1 tablespoon Thai red curry paste

1 tablespoon fish sauce

1 egg, beaten

2 teaspoons brown sugar

1 clove garlic, crushed

4 kaffir lime leaves, finely shredded, or
   2 teaspoons grated lime zest (rind)

2 tablespoons chopped fresh cilantro (fresh
   coriander)

2 scallions (shallots/spring onions), finely sliced

$\frac{1}{2}$ cup (2$\frac{1}{2}$ oz/75 g) finely sliced green beans

3 tablespoons vegetable oil, for frying

12 bamboo skewers

$\frac{1}{2}$ cup (4 fl oz/125 ml) light soy sauce, for dipping

lime wedges and extra skewers, for serving

Place fish fillets, curry paste, fish sauce, egg, sugar and garlic in a food processor. Process until mixture forms a thick paste, about 20 seconds. Transfer to a bowl. Add lime leaves, cilantro, scallions and beans. Using wet hands, mix until well combined. Form mixture into 36 balls. Flatten each to form a patty shape.

Warm oil in a frying pan over medium heat. Working in batches, fry fish cakes until golden, about 1 minute on each side. Remove fish cakes from pan and drain on paper towels, then place 3 fish cakes on each skewer.

Serve with soy sauce for dipping and fresh lime wedges on skewers for garnish.

Makes 36 cakes

Hints

Fish cake mixture can be prepared 2 hours ahead.

Keep covered and refrigerated.

CILANTRO AND LIME FISH CAKES

Cucumber disks with chili shrimp

2 scallions (shallots/spring onions) (see page 9
  for step-by-step scallion curls)
1 lemon (see page 8 for step-by-step zesting)
1 lime
3 large English (hothouse) cucumbers
20 medium cooked shrimp (prawns), peeled and
  deveined, tails intact
¼ cup (2 fl oz/60 ml) Thai sweet chili sauce

Trim away root end of scallions. Cut scallions into 1-inch (2.5-cm) lengths, then slice lengthwise into long, thin shreds. Place in a bowl of ice water to curl, about 10 minutes. Dry on paper towels. Using a zester, remove zest from lemon and lime in long, fine strips. Slice cucumber into rounds ½ inch (12 mm) thick. Trim to make uniform rounds using a 1½-inch (4-cm) cookie (pastry) cutter. This will also remove peel.

Place cucumber rounds on a serving platter. Top each with a shrimp, then drizzle with chili sauce and garnish with scallion curls and lemon and lime strips.

Makes 20

Hints

Prepare scallion curls and zest strips, and peel and devein shrimp 1 hour ahead. Keep these ingredients covered and refrigerated. Assemble the dish just before serving.

Pears and prosciutto on grilled bread

½ loaf wood-fired bread

3 tablespoons olive oil, for brushing

2 firm, but ripe, pears

10 thin slices prosciutto

4 oz (125 g) roquefort or other blue cheese

small arugula (rocket) leaves, for garnish

Preheat broiler (grill). Using a serrated knife, thinly slice bread, then trim into 20 serving-sized pieces about 2½ inches (6 cm) square. Brush both sides of bread lightly with oil. Place in broiler (grill) and toast on both sides until golden, 1–2 minutes.

Slice pears lengthwise and trim to fit bread pieces. Brush pear slices with oil, place in broiler (grill) and cook until slightly softened, about 1 minute on each side.

Cut prosciutto slices in half. Top each toasted bread slice with a prosciutto slice, a pear slice and a little crumbled cheese. Garnish with an arugula leaf.

Makes 20

Hints

Toast bread 1 hour ahead. Use rustic or country bread if wood-fired bread is unavailable.

Cilantro and shrimp toasts

12 large slices stale white sandwich bread

2 scallions (shallots/spring onions), chopped

2 cloves garlic, crushed

1 teaspoon peeled and grated fresh ginger

8 oz (250 g) jumbo shrimp (green king prawns),
  peeled and deveined

1 tablespoon cornstarch

1 teaspoon soy sauce

2 tablespoons chopped fresh cilantro (fresh
  coriander)

1 egg yolk

2 teaspoons sesame seeds

3 cups (24 fl oz/750 ml) vegetable oil, for frying

Using a 2-inch (5-cm) cookie (pastry) cutter, cut 2 rounds from each slice of bread. Place scallions, garlic, ginger, shrimp, cornstarch, soy sauce and cilantro in a food processor. Process until mixture forms a thick paste, about 15 seconds. Brush one side of each bread round with egg yolk, then spread with 1 teaspoon shrimp mixture. Sprinkle with sesame seeds.

Heat oil in a deep, heavy-bottomed saucepan or deep-fat fryer until it reaches 375°F (190°C) on a deep-frying thermometer or until a small cube of bread dropped into the oil sizzles and turns golden. Working in batches, deep-fry bread rounds in hot oil until golden and crisp on both sides, 1–2 minutes total. Remove bread rounds from pan and drain on paper towels.

Serve immediately.

Makes 24

Hints

Shrimp mixture can be prepared 2 hours ahead.

Keep mixture covered and refrigerated.

CILANTRO AND SHRIMP TOASTS

Herbed egg tartlets

2 sheets frozen shortcrust pastry, thawed

1 tablespoon butter

4 eggs, beaten

2 tablespoons chopped mixed herbs such as
  thyme, parsley, sage, marjoram and dill

¹/₄ cup (2 fl oz/60 ml) milk

1 oz (30 g) black lumpfish caviar

Preheat oven to 375°F (190°C/Gas 5). Place pastry sheets on a work surface and cut out 24 rounds using a 2½-inch (6-cm) cookie (pastry) cutter. Line greased mini muffin pans with pastry. Bake in preheated oven until golden, about 12 minutes. Remove pans from oven and set aside.

In a saucepan, melt butter, then add eggs, herbs and milk. Cook over medium heat, without stirring, until mixture bubbles. Gently stir (only 6–8 times) with a fork. Cook until firm but not overcooked, 2–3 minutes more. If eggs become very rubbery and start to "weep", they are overcooked. Remove saucepan from heat and allow eggs to cool slightly.

Spoon eggs into warm pastry cups, top with lumpfish caviar and serve immediately.

Makes about 24

Hints

Baked pastry cups can be made 1 day ahead. Store in an airtight container and reheat before serving. They can also be frozen for up to 1 month. The eggs are best made just before serving.

Ham rarebit toasts with dill pickle

2 tablespoon olive oil

3 tablespoons butter, softened

2 tablespoons grainy mustard

1 ciabatta or other loaf of heavy white bread

8 oz (250 g) shaved ham

4 oz (125 g) sharp (tasty) cheese, thinly sliced

freshly ground black pepper to taste

8 dill pickles (pickled cucumbers), cut into

  quarters or

32 mini pickles

Preheat oven to 400°F (200°C/Gas 6). Combine oil, butter and mustard in a small bowl. Using a serrated knife, cut bread slices each about ½ inch (12 mm) thick. If using ciabatta, cut bread into quarters. Brush one side of each slice of bread with butter mixture. Place on parchment-lined (baking paper–lined) baking sheets, buttered side up. Bake in preheated oven until golden and crisp, 5–8 minutes.

Preheat broiler (grill). Place a little ham on each toast slice, then top with a slice of cheese. Place under broiler until cheese melts.

To serve, grind a little pepper on top, and add pickle.

Makes 32

HAM RAREBIT TOASTS WITH DILL PICKLE

Palmiers and pinwheels

2 sheets pre-rolled frozen puff pastry, thawed

$1/_3$ cup ($2^1/_2$ oz/75 g) Tapenade (see recipe page 104) or

$1/_3$ cup ($2^1/_2$ oz/75 g) Pesto (see recipe page 102)

2 teaspoons sea salt

Preheat oven to 400°F (200°C/Gas 6). Place pastry sheets on work surface. Spread on pesto or tapenade, evenly covering the pastry.

To make palmiers: Roll one side of sheet to center and other side to center to meet the first. Turn and cut crosswise with a sharp knife into ½-inch (12-mm) slices. Place palmiers on parchment-lined (baking paper–lined) baking sheets, cut side up. Sprinkle with sea salt.

To make pinwheels: Roll sheet in one direction only. Cut into ½-inch (12-mm) slices. Place on parchment-lined (baking paper–lined) baking sheets and sprinkle with sea salt.

Bake palmiers and pinwheels in preheated oven until golden and crisp, 7–10 minutes. Remove from oven and allow to cool on baking sheets.

Makes 35–40

Hints

You can use a supermarket or delicatessen variety of prepared pesto, tapenade or sun-dried tomato pesto to save time. The palmiers and pinwheels are best made on the same day as serving.

Mascarpone and fruit tartlets

2 sheets frozen shortcrust pastry, thawed

8 oz (250 g) soft mascarpone

6½ oz (200 g) blueberries, picked over

6½ oz (200 g) strawberries, hulls removed, sliced

2 tablespoons confectioners' (icing) sugar, sifted

Preheat oven to 375°F (190°C/Gas 5). Place pastry on work surface and cut 24 rounds using a 2½-inch (6-cm) cookie (pastry) cutter. Line greased mini muffin pans with pastry rounds. Bake until golden, about 12 minutes. Remove pans from oven and turn pastry cups onto a wire rack and allow to cool.

In a small bowl, beat mascarpone with a wooden spoon until smooth and pliable. Spoon 2 teaspoons mascarpone into each cup.

Arrange berries attractively over mascarpone and dust with sugar just before serving.

Makes 24

Hints

Pastry cups can be made 1 day ahead. They can be stored in an airtight container, or kept frozen for up to 1 month.

MASCARPONE AND FRUIT TARTLETS

Fairy ice-cream sandwiches

4 oz (125 g) butter, softened

1/2 cup (3 1/2 oz/105 g) superfine sugar (caster sugar)

1 egg, beaten

1 1/2 cups (7 1/2 oz/235 g) self-rising flour, sifted

2 tablespoons cocoa

2 cups (16 fl oz/500 ml) vanilla or strawberry ice cream

Preheat oven to 350°F (180°C/Gas 4). Place butter and sugar in a bowl. Using a mixer, beat until soft and creamy, about 3 minutes. Add egg and beat well. Fold in sifted flour and cocoa. Turn mixture out on a floured work surface and knead lightly until smooth. With a rolling pin, roll mixture between 2 sheets of parchment (baking paper) until about ¼ inch (6 mm) thick. Using a 2-inch (5-cm) cookie (pastry) cutter, cut 32 rounds. Place rounds on parchment-lined (baking paper–lined) baking sheets and bake in preheated oven until firm to the touch, 10–12 minutes. Remove from oven and allow to cool on baking sheets.

Working quickly and in small batches, sandwich 2 rounds together with a scoop of ice cream. Wrap sandwiches individually in plastic wrap and place in freezer.

Freeze for at least 2 hours before serving.

Makes 16

Hints

Can be made 1 week ahead. Sandwiches can be stored in an airtight container in the freezer. Remove from freezer just before serving.

FAIRY ICE-CREAM SANDWICHES

Raspberry madeleines

2 large eggs

¹/₂ cup (3¹/₂ oz/105 g) superfine sugar (caster sugar)

3¹/₂ oz (105 g) all-purpose (plain) flour, sifted

¹/₄ teaspoon baking powder

pinch sea salt

3¹/₂ oz (105 g) butter, melted and cooled

¹/₂ teaspoon vanilla extract (essence)

35 raspberries

35 toothpicks

1 tablespoon confectioners' (icing) sugar, sifted

Preheat oven to 350°F (180°C/Gas 4). Place eggs and sugar in a bowl. Using a mixer, beat until thick and creamy, about 7 minutes. Fold in sifted flour, baking powder and salt. Add butter and vanilla, and gently fold in. Spoon 1 teaspoon of batter into each mold of greased mini madeleine (shell) pans (each mold should be ¾ full). Bake in preheated oven until golden and risen, about 20 minutes. Remove pans from oven, and turn madeleines out onto a wire rack to cool.

Skewer a raspberry to each madeleine with a toothpick. Dust with confectioners' sugar before serving.

Makes 35

Hints

Best made same day as serving. Measure the flour carefully before sifting.

RASPBERRY MADELEINES

Choc-almond apricots

6½ oz (200 g) dark chocolate, chopped

36 large whole plump dried apricots

36 whole blanched almonds

Place chocolate in a heatproof bowl or in top pan of a double boiler. Place bowl over saucepan of simmering water. Stir until chocolate melts, 3–4 minutes. Remove from heat. Allow to stand 5 minutes.

Using your fingers or a fork, dip half of each apricot into melted chocolate. Place on a plate lined with parchment (baking paper). Top with an almond. Repeat with remaining ingredients. Refrigerate until chocolate is firm, about 15 minutes.

Serve with coffee.

Makes 36

Hints

Can be made 1 week ahead. Store in airtight container in refrigerator.

CHOC-ALMOND APRICOTS

Pesto

1 cup (1½ oz/45 g) well-packed basil leaves

2 oz (60 g) pine nuts, toasted

2 cloves garlic, chopped

pinch sea salt

juice of 1 lemon

2 oz (60 g) grated parmesan

½ cup (4 fl oz/125 ml) extra virgin olive oil

Place basil, pine nuts, garlic, salt, lemon juice and parmesan in a food processor. Process until well blended, about 15 seconds. With food processor running, gradually add oil. Process until pesto has the consistency of thick paste. Store in an airtight container in the refrigerator for up to 3 weeks.

Makes 1 cup (8 oz/250 g)

Hints

Substitute arugula (rocket) leaves for half of the basil for a taste variation. Serve as a spread on crostini, grilled vegetables, or oven-roasted potatoes.

Tapenade

14 oz (440g) pitted black olives

2 tablespoons capers

4 oz (125 g) anchovy fillets, drained

Place olives, capers and anchovies in a food processor and process until mixture becomes a thick paste, about 10 seconds. Store in an airtight container in the refrigerator for up to 3 weeks.

Add chopped red chili pepper for a spicy-hot tapenade variation.

Makes 1 cup (8 oz/250 g)

Taramasalata

1/2 small white onion

1 cup (2 oz/60 g) well-packed soft white stale breadcrumbs

1 tablespoon strained lemon juice

1/3 cup (3 fl oz/90 ml) olive oil

1 clove garlic, crushed

1 egg yolk

2 oz (60 g) fish roe

Grate onion into a bowl and strain through a fine sieve, pressing firmly to extract juice. In a bowl, combine 2 teaspoons of onion juice, breadcrumbs, lemon juice and olive oil. Cover and allow to stand until bread becomes soft, about 15 minutes. Add garlic and beat, using a mixer. Beat in egg yolk, then gradually add fish roe, beating until light and fluffy. If mixture is too thick, add a little more lemon juice. Store in an airtight container in the refrigerator. Keeps well for up to 3 days.

Serve as a dip with crusty bread, radishes, and celery sticks.

Glossary

anchovy fillets: Canned or bottled anchovy fillets come either flat or rolled around a caper and packed in oil. Some people prefer to rinse anchovies in water or soak them in milk for 20 minutes to give them a milder, less salty flavor.

balsamic vinegar: Rich, strong-flavored reddish brown vinegar, made from unfermented grape juice. The finest balsamic vinegars are very costly, like good wine.

blanched almonds: The nut of the almond tree, from which the skins have been removed. Available whole, sliced or slivered.

bocconcini: Small rounds of fresh mozzarella cheese about 1 inch (2.5 cm) in diameter, packed in water or whey to keep them moist. Sold in containers. The slightly acid, walnut-flavored cheeses are often served with tomatoes and basil.

buttermilk: Made commercially from nonfat or lowfat milk and fortified with milk solids, to which a benign culture of acid-producing bacteria has been added. Buttermilk has a pleasant, light tang and a thick, creamy consistency.

cannellini beans: Large, elongated kidney-shaped beans, creamy white in color, traditionally used in soups and salads. Also known as white kidney beans.

cellophane noodles: Thin, translucent dried noodles made from mung bean starch and sold in bundles. Also called bean thread noodles.

chervil: A ferny-leafed herb that resembles parsley and tastes like aniseed. Fresh chervil can be stored for up to 1 week in a plastic bag in the refrigerator.

Chinese roast duck: Sold freshly roasted at Chinese markets. Delicious on its own or in fillings or salads. Use 1–2 days after purchase. Substitute roast chicken if unavailable.

chorizo: A spiced, coarsely textured cured sausage, originally from Spain. Made from pork, pork fat, garlic and paprika.

cilantro: Pungent, fragrant leaves from the coriander plant, resembling parsley and also called Chinese parsley or fresh coriander. Fresh cilantro can be stored for up to 1 week in a plastic bag in the refrigerator.

crème fraîche: A cultured cream product, with a tart, tangy flavor similar to sour cream but thinner in texture. Use sour cream if crème fraîche is unavailable.

crostini: Italian for "little toasts". Used to describe small, thin slices of toasted bread, often lightly brushed with olive oil.

fish sauce: Bottled sauce derived from salted fermented fish along with other seasonings and used in moderation to add pungent flavor to dressings, dipping sauces and other recipes. Sauces can vary in intensity depending on country of origin. Fish sauce from Thailand, called nam pla, is a commonly available variety.

flat-leaf parsley: Parsley with a flat leaf and a stronger flavor than curly-leafed parsley. Also known as Italian or Continental parsley. Fresh parsley can be stored for up to 1 week in a plastic bag in the refrigerator.

flour tortilla: A round, thin, unleavened Mexican bread made from masa or wheat flour.

hoisin sauce: Sweet, thick Chinese sauce made from soybeans, vinegar, sugar, chili peppers and other seasonings. Bottled hoisin sauce can be stored indefinitely in the refrigerator.

hollandaise sauce: One of the great basic sauces: a rich mixture of butter and egg yolks, seasoned with lemon juice. Sold prepared in some stores and delicatessens.

kaffir lime leaves: Leaves from the kaffir lime tree, often used dried but also used fresh to add an appealing citrus flavor to a variety of Asian dishes.

lumpfish caviar: Harvested from the lumpfish, the small fish eggs are usually dyed black, red or gold. They are also known as Danish caviar.

mascarpone: A luscious cheese made from cow's milk. It has the consistency of butter and a sweet, slightly acidic flavor.

pappadams (Baby): Thin, crisp wafers made from spiced lentil, potato or rice flour, traditionally eaten with curries and Indian foods. Pappadams are available in various flavors and sizes, from Asian markets and many grocery stores.

polenta: Dried, ground corn kernels, white or yellow in color, with a gritty texture and a slightly sweet, starchy flavor. Available in fine, medium and coarse grinds.

prosciutto: A ham that has been cured by salting and then drying in the air. It is also known as Parma ham.

rice paper wrappers: Dried rice-based wrappers, available in different sizes from Asian markets and many grocery stores. To reconstitute rice paper wrappers, soak them in hot water for 15 seconds.

roquefort: A veined cheese made from sheep's milk and ripened in the limestone caves at Roquefort, in southern France. Creamy-colored with blue–green veining. Use any other blue vein cheese if unavailable.

rosemary: An extremely fragrant evergreen herb with spiky leaves and pale blue flowers. Use fresh rosemary sparingly, as it has a strong flavor.

sake: A clear Japanese wine made from fermented rice.

salmon roe: Roe harvested from chum or silver salmon. The large eggs have an orange color.

scallion: Bulbless onion with long green leaves. Also known as shallot or green onion.

tapas: Spanish appetizers, sometimes served to constitute a whole meal.

Thai red curry paste: A ready-made paste, made from Asian ingredients and spices. Available from most grocery stores and Asian markets.

wonton wrapper: Thin sheets of wheat-based or egg-based dough, square or circular in shape, used to enclose a variety of fillings. Available fresh or frozen. Also called wonton skins or dumpling wrappers.

Index

Almonds, salt-and-spice 12
Anchovy-filled zucchini flowers 56
Apricots, choc-almond 100
Asian rolls, fresh 11
Asian spring rolls, fresh 76
Asparagus
    frittata 62
    ham and hollandaise rolls 50

Basil pesto 102
Bean dip with herb toast fingers 28
Black olive tapenade 104
Blini bites with salmon roe 34
Bocconcini, cherry tomato and basil skewers 68
Butter, herb and garlic 44

Cheese
    cherry tomato, bocconcini and basil skewers 68
    herbed, with endive leaves and walnuts 46
    parmesan stars and hearts 16
    parmesan wafers 18
Cherry tomato, bocconcini and basil skewers 68
Chicken
    drummettes 40
    yakitori 64
Chicory (endive) leaves with herbed cheese and walnuts 46
Chili-herb shrimp 70
Chilled gazpacho sips 54
Chips, fresh vegetable 14
Choc-almond apricots 100
Chorizo on crostini 20
Cilantro
    and lime fish cakes 80
    and shrimp toasts 86

Continental sausage rolls 52
Coriander see Cilantro
Corn-and-herb muffins, petite 44
Courgette (zucchini) flowers, anchovy-filled 56
Crepes, asparagus, ham and hollandaise 50
Crisp vegetable chips 14
Crostini, warm chorizo on 20
Cucumber disks with chili shrimp 82
Curried mango dip 30

Dip
    curried mango 30
    skordalia 32
    tapenade 104
    taramasalata 104
    white bean, with herb toast fingers 28
Duck rolls, tiny Peking 74
Dumplings, steamed shrimp and spinach 78

Egg tartlets, herbed (warm) 88
Endive leaves with herbed cheese and walnuts 46

Fairy ice-cream sandwiches 96
Figs, fresh, wrapped in prosciutto 48
Fish
    cakes, cilantro and lime 80
    smoked trout pâté 24
    tuna with green olive salsa 60
Fish roe
    blini bites with salmon roe 34
    lumpfish caviar with oven-roasted potatoes 22
    taramasalata 104
Fresh Asian rolls 11

Fresh Asian spring rolls 76
Fresh figs wrapped in prosciutto 48
Frittata, asparagus 62
Fruit and mascarpone tartlets 94

Garlic-chilli green olives 12
Gazpacho sips, chilled 54
Green olives
    garlic-chili 12
    salsa 60

Ham
    asparagus and hollandaise rolls 50
    rarebit toasts with dill pickle 90
Herb and garlic butter 44
Herb polenta baked in prosciutto 66
Herb toast fingers 28
Herbed (warm) egg tartlets 88

Ice-cream sandwiches, fairy 96

Lamb and potatoes, skewered 72
Lemon zest curls 8
Lime zest curls 8
Lumpfish caviar with oven-roasted potatoes 22

Madeleines, raspberry 98
Mango dip, curried 30
Mascarpone and fruit tartlets 94
Melon and prosciutto wraps 48
Mini pissaladière 38
Muffins, petite corn-and-herb 44

Olives
    garlic-chili 12
    salsa 60
    tapenade 104
Onion-and-chervil scones 36

Oven-roasted potatoes with lumpfish caviar 22
Oysters in bacon 20

Palmiers 92
Parmesan
    stars and hearts 16
    wafers 18
Pâté
    potted shrimp 26
    smoked trout 24
Pears and prosciutto on grilled bread 84
Peking duck rolls, tiny 74
Pesto 102
Petite corn-and-herb muffins 44
Phyllo-wrapped shrimp with taramasalata 58
Pinwheels 92
Pissaladière, mini 38
Polenta, herb, baked in prosciutto 66
Potatoes
    and lamb, skewered 72
    oven-roasted, with lumpfish caviar 22
    skordalia 32
Potted shrimp 26
Prawns see Shrimp
Prosciutto
    fresh figs wrapped in 48
    herb polenta baked in 66
    and melon wraps 48
    and pears on grilled bread 84

Raspberry madeleines 98
Ricotta, herbed, with endive leaves and walnuts 46
Roe see Fish roe
Rolls, fresh Asian 11

Salmon roe with blini bites 34
Salsa, green olive 60
Salt-and-spice almonds 12
Sausages

continental rolls 52

warm chorizo on crostini 20

Scallion brushes and curls 9

Scones, onion-and-chervil 36

Shallot (scallion) brushes and curls 9

Shrimp

chili-herb 70

chili, with cucumber disks 82

and cilantro toasts 86

phyllo-wrapped, with taramasalata 58

potted 26

and spinach dumplings, steamed 78

Skewered lamb and potatoes 72

Skordalia 32

Smoked trout pâté 24

Spinach and shrimp dumplings, steamed 78

Spring onion (scallion) brushes and curls 9

Spring rolls, fresh Asian 76

Steamed shrimp and spinach dumplings 78

Sun-dried tomato-filled toast cups 42

Tapenade 104

Taramasalata 104

with phyllo-wrapped shrimp 58

Tartlets

herbed (warm) egg 88

mascarpone and fruit 94

mini pissaladière 38

Tiny Peking duck rolls 74

Toast

cilantro and shrimp 86

cups 10

cups, sun-dried tomato-filled 42

ham rarebit, with dill pickle 90

herb fingers 28

whole-grain triangles 26

Tomato

bocconcini and basil skewers 68

toast cups 42

Trout pâté, smoked 24

Tuna with green olive salsa 60

Vegetable chips 14

Warm chorizo on crostini 20

White bean dip with herb toast fingers 28

Whole-grain toast triangles 26

Witloof (endive) leaves with herbed cheese and walnuts 46

Zest curls 8

Zucchini flowers, anchovy-filled 56

Guide to weights and measures

The conversions given in the recipes in this book are approximate. Whichever system you use, remember to follow it consistently, thereby ensuring that the proportions are consistent throughout a recipe.

WEIGHTS

Imperial	Metric
⅓ oz	10 g
½ oz	15 g
¾ oz	20 g
1 oz	30 g
2 oz	60 g
3 oz	90 g
4 oz (¼ lb)	125 g
5 oz (⅓ lb)	150 g
6 oz	180 g
7 oz	220 g
8 oz (½ lb)	250 g
9 oz	280 g
10 oz	300 g
11 oz	330 g
12 oz (¾ lb)	375 g
16 oz (1 lb)	500 g
2 lb	1 kg
3 lb	1.5 kg
4 lb	2 kg

USEFUL CONVERSIONS

¼ teaspoon	1.25 ml
½ teaspoon	2.5 ml
1 teaspoon	5 ml
1 Australian tablespoon	20 ml (4 teaspoons)
1 UK/US tablespoon	15 ml (3 teaspoons)

Butter/Shortening

1 tablespoon	½ oz	15 g
1½ tablespoons	¾ oz	20 g
2 tablespoons	1 oz	30 g
3 tablespoons	1 ½ oz	45 g

OVEN TEMPERATURE GUIDE

The Celsius (°C) and Fahrenheit (°F) temperatures in this chart apply to most electric ovens. Decrease by 25°F or 10°C for a gas oven or refer to the manufacturer's temperature guide. For temperatures below 325°F (160°C), do not decrease the given temperature.

VOLUME

Imperial	Metric	Cup
1 fl oz	30 ml	
2 fl oz	60 ml	¼
3	90 ml	⅓
4	125 ml	½
5	150 ml	⅔
6	180 ml	¾
8	250 ml	1
10	300 ml	1¼
12	375 ml	1½
13	400 ml	1⅔
14	440 ml	1¾
16	500 ml	2
24	750 ml	3
32	1L	4

Oven description	°C	°F	Gas Mark
Cool	110	225	¼
	130	250	½
Very slow	140	275	1
	150	300	2
Slow	170	325	3
Moderate	180	350	4
	190	375	5
Moderately Hot	200	400	6
Fairly Hot	220	425	7
Hot	230	450	8
Very Hot	240	475	9
Extremely Hot	250	500	10

First published in the United States in 2000 by Periplus Editions (HK) Ltd.,
with editorial offices at 153 Milk Street, Boston, Massachusetts 02109 and
5 Little Road #08-01 Singapore 536983

Library of Congress Cataloging-in-Publication Data is available.
ISBN 962-593-820-6

DISTRIBUTED BY

USA
Tuttle Publishing
Distribution Center
Airport Industrial Park
364 Innovation Drive
North Clarendon, VT 05759-9436
Tel: (802) 773-8930
Tel: (800) 526-2778

Japan
Tuttle Publishing
RK Building, 2nd Floor
2-13-10 Shimo-Meguro, Meguro-Ku
Tokyo 153 0064
Tel: (03) 5437-0171
Fax: (03) 5437-0755

Canada
Raincoast Books
8680 Cambie Street
Vancouver, British Colombia
V6P 6M9
Tel: (604) 323 7100
Fax: (604) 323 2600

Southeast Asia
Berkeley Books Pte. Ltd.
5 Little Road #08-01
Singapore 53698
Tel: (65) 280-3320
Fax: (65) 280-6290

Set in Frutiger on QuarkXPress
Printed in Singapore

First Edition
06 05 04 03 02 01 00 10 9 8 7 6 5 4 3 2 1